THE PHILANTHROPIC MINDSET:

How to Give Smart and Live Rich

ADELLA PASOS

Contents

Introduction

Giving to charity is a noble and fulfilling endeavor, but it can also be overwhelming and confusing. With so many worthy causes and organizations to choose from, it can be difficult to know where to focus your resources to make the most impact. This book provides a framework for making philanthropic decisions that align with your values and goals, so you can give with confidence and purpose.

This book begins by exploring the concept of the philanthropic mindset and the importance of having a clear vision for your giving. It then provides techniques for creating a philanthropic plan that fits your lifestyle and goals, as well as strategies for evaluating the effectiveness of different charitable organizations and causes. Throughout the book, you will learn how to measure and track the impact of their philanthropy, and how to involve their family and community in their giving.

One of the key themes of this book is the idea of giving smarter, rather than just giving more. You'll learn the importance of balancing short-term and long-term goals, and how to think strategically about how to leverage their resources, including time, money, and connections, for maximum impact. This book also provides ideas for how to give in a way that brings joy and fulfillment to both the giver and the recipients of the generosity.

Overall, "The Philanthropic Mindset" is a comprehensive guide to making a difference in the world while also living the life you want. Whether you're a seasoned philanthropist or just getting started, this book will provide you with the tools and inspiration you need to give smart and live rich.

Overview of Philanthropy

Philanthropy is the practice of giving money, time, or resources to organizations or causes that aim to make a positive impact in the world. Philanthropy can take many forms, from donating money to charitable organizations to volunteering time to causes you care about, to name a few. Philanthropy can also include impact investing, social enterprise and other forms of strategic giving.

In terms of the short-term benefits, philanthropy can provide a sense of fulfillment and purpose, as well as the satisfaction of knowing that you are making a positive difference in the world. It can also be a way to connect with others who share your values and passions, and to build a sense of community around a common cause.

In the long-term, philanthropy can help you achieve your personal and professional goals, as well as contribute to the common good. It can be a way to leave a lasting legacy, and to make a meaningful impact on the world long after you're gone. Furthermore, Philanthropy can also be a way of addressing social and environmental issues that align with your values and goals, and contribute to building a better future for all.

By incorporating philanthropy into your life, you can not only help others but also benefit yourself. It allows you to align your values, goals, and resources to make a real difference in the world and create a more meaningful and fulfilling life for yourself.

Why is Philanthropy is Important

Philanthropy is a way for people of all income levels to make a difference in the world, to address social and economic disparities, to shape their communities, and to benefit themselves. It is a tool for everyone to use to make the world a better place and to create a more meaningful and fulfilling life for themselves.

Philanthropy is important for both the wealthy and the unwealthy alike for several reasons:

1. Philanthropy is a way for everyone to make a difference, regardless of their financial resources. People of all income levels can give their time, skills, and expertise to causes they care about, and there are many ways to give that don't require a lot of money.

2. Philanthropy helps to address social and economic disparities by providing resources and support to communities and individuals in need. Philanthropy can be used to fund programs and services that serve marginalized communities, and can help to reduce poverty and inequality.

3. Philanthropy allows individuals to take an active role in shaping their communities and the world around them. It is a way for people to express their values and to make a positive impact on the issues they care about.

4. Philanthropy is also important for the wealthy, as it allows them to use their resources to make a significant impact on society. Wealthy individuals and foundations can make large-scale donations and grants that can change the lives of many people for the better.

5. Philanthropy can also have a positive impact on the giver, regardless of wealth. It can provide a sense of purpose and fulfillment, and can be a way to connect with others and build a sense of community.

CHAPTER 1

The Basics of Philanthropy

Philanthropy is the practice of giving money, time, or resources to organizations or causes that aim to make a positive impact in the world. Philanthropy can take many forms, from donating money to charitable organizations to volunteering time to causes you care about, to name a few.

One of the most common forms of philanthropy is monetary donations to charitable organizations. These organizations may focus on a wide range of issues, such as poverty, education, health care, and the environment. Donors can choose to give to a specific organization or cause, or they can give to a charitable foundation that distributes funds to multiple organizations.

Another form of philanthropy is volunteering time and skills to a cause or organization. This can include mentoring young people, working on a community service project, or serving on the board of a nonprofit organization.

In addition, Impact investing and social enterprise are becoming a more popular form of philanthropy. Impact investing is an investment strategy that seeks to generate a measurable, beneficial social or environmental impact alongside a financial return. Social enterprise refers to a business model where the primary goal is to create a positive social or environmental impact.

When considering philanthropy, it's important to align your values and passions with the causes or organizations you choose to support. It's also important to evaluate the effectiveness of the organizations you're considering, by looking at factors such as their financial stability, transparency, and impact.

Overall, philanthropy is a way for individuals and organizations to make a positive impact in the world, while also aligning their values and goals. It can take many forms, from monetary donations to volunteering time and skills, and it's open to everyone regardless of their financial resources. Philanthropy is a powerful tool for creating a better world, and for building a more meaningful and fulfilling life for oneself.

Creating a plan for philanthropy is an important first step in making a meaningful and impactful difference in the world. Here are some of the first steps you can take in creating your own philanthropy plan:

- **Identify your values and passions**: Start by thinking about the issues and causes that align with your values and passions. What do you care about most deeply and why? What kind of impact do you want to make in the world?

- **Research potential causes and organizations:** Once you have identified your values and passions, research different causes and organizations that align with them. Look for information on the organization's mission, impact, and financial stability.

- **Assess your resources:** Consider how much time, money, and other resources you have available to give. This will help you determine what type of giving is most appropriate for you and how much you can realistically give.

- **Create a budget:** Create a budget for your giving that includes both short-term and long-term goals. Be realistic about what you can afford to give while also considering your long-term financial plans.

- **Set clear and measurable goals:** Set specific, measurable goals for your giving. This will help you track your progress and measure the impact of your philanthropy.

- **Be flexible and adaptable:** Be prepared to make adjustments to your plan as you learn more about the organizations and causes you support. Be open to new opportunities and be willing to re-evaluate your goals and priorities as needed.

By following these steps, you can create a philanthropy plan that aligns with your values, passions and resources, and allows you to make a meaningful and measurable impact in the world. Remember to keep an open mind and be flexible as you navigate through your philanthropic journey.

The Importance of Having a Philanthropic Mindset

Having a philanthropic mindset is essential for making a meaningful and impactful difference in the world. A philanthropic mindset is characterized by a commitment to giving back to others, a desire to make a positive impact in the world, and a willingness to be strategic and intentional in your giving.

One of the key benefits of having a philanthropic mindset is that it allows you to align your values and passions with your giving. By taking the time to identify what you care about most deeply, you can focus your resources on causes and organizations that align with your values, which will increase the impact of your giving.

Another important aspect of having a philanthropic mindset is being strategic and intentional in your giving. This means taking the time to research different causes and organizations, evaluating their effectiveness and impact, and setting clear and measurable goals for your giving. It also means being open to new opportunities, and being willing to adjust your giving plan as you learn more about the organizations and causes you support.

Having a philanthropic mindset also means being open to new ways of giving. Philanthropy can take many forms, from monetary donations to volunteering time and skills, and it's open to everyone regardless of their financial resources. A philanthropic mindset also means being open to impact investing, social enterprise, and other forms of strategic giving.

Having a philanthropic mindset can also have a positive impact on the giver, as it can provide a sense of purpose and fulfillment, and can be a way to connect with others and build a sense of community.

Having a philanthropic mindset is essential for making a meaningful and impactful difference in the world. It allows you to align your values and passions with your giving, to be strategic and intentional in your giving, to be open to new ways of giving, and can have a positive impact on the giver. By cultivating a philanthropic mindset, you can create a more meaningful and fulfilling life for yourself while making a difference in the world.

Is it better to give money or time?

Both giving money and giving time can make a meaningful difference, and the best approach may be to give a combination of both.

One of the main advantages of giving money is that it can be a flexible and efficient way to support causes and organizations. Money can be used to fund specific programs, projects, or general operations, and can be directed to where it is needed most. Giving money can also be a way to leverage the expertise and resources of organizations that are already working on a particular issue or cause, allowing them to scale their impact.

On the other hand, giving time can be a more personal and direct way to make a difference. This can include volunteering, mentoring, or participating in community projects. Giving time can also be a way to build relationships and connections with the community, and can provide a sense of fulfillment and purpose. Additionally, giving time can be a way to gain skills, knowledge, and experience, which can be valuable for personal and professional growth.

It's worth noting that giving money or time doesn't have to be an either/or decision. Many people choose to give a combination of both, which can have the best of both worlds. For example, a philanthropist could give money to an organization to support its operations and also volunteer their time to support the organization's programs.

Additionally, the choice of giving money or time may also depend on the resources the individual has available. For example, some people may not have the financial resources to give money, but may have the time and skills to volunteer. On the other hand, some people may not have the time to volunteer, but may have the financial resources to give money.

How do I volunteer effectively?

Volunteering can be a powerful way to make a difference in the world and can be a fulfilling and rewarding experience. Here are some steps you can take to volunteer effectively:

1. **Identify your interests and skills:** Before you start volunteering, it's important to think about the causes and issues that you are passionate about and the skills and abilities you can bring to the table. This will help you identify volunteer opportunities that align with your interests and skills.

2. **Research volunteer opportunities:** Once you have identified your interests and skills, research different volunteer opportunities that align with them. This can include looking at volunteer listings on websites, contacting nonprofit organizations directly, or reaching out to friends and family who may know of volunteer opportunities.

3. **Interview the organization:** Before committing to a volunteer opportunity, it's important to speak with the organization to understand their mission, goals, and the specific volunteer role you would be filling. This can help you determine whether the opportunity aligns with your interests and skills and whether it would be a good fit for you.

4. **Set clear expectations:** Once you have committed to a volunteer opportunity, set clear expectations with the organization about your role, responsibilities, and time commitment. This can help ensure that your volunteer experience is productive and satisfying for both you and the organization.

5. **Show up and be reliable:** Once you start volunteering, it's important to show up on time and be reliable. This can help build trust with the organization and ensure that the volunteer work is getting done.

6. **Communicate and be open to feedback:** During your volunteer experience, it's important to communicate with the organization and be open to feedback. This can help ensure that you are meeting the organization's expectations and that you are making a positive impact.

7. **Reflect on your experience:** After your volunteer experience, take the time to reflect on your experience and what you have learned. This can help you identify areas where you excelled and areas where you can improve. It can also help you decide if you would like to continue volunteering with the same organization or explore other volunteer opportunities.

8. **Be flexible:** Be open to new experiences and be willing to try different roles and tasks. Being flexible can help you discover

new passions and skills, and it can also help the organization as they may have urgent needs that need to be addressed.

9. **Follow-up:** Keep in touch with the organization after your volunteer experience. This can help build a relationship and can also open up new opportunities for future volunteer work.

10. **Give back in different ways:** Volunteering doesn't always have to be done in person, there are many ways to give back such as through online volunteer work, donating goods, and participating in fundraising events.

It's worth noting that volunteering can be a challenging and rewarding experience, and it's important to find the right opportunity that aligns with your interests, skills, and values. Additionally, it's important to set realistic expectations and to be prepared for the challenges that come with volunteering.

Volunteering can be a powerful way to make a difference in the world and can be a fulfilling and rewarding experience. By identifying your interests and skills, researching volunteer opportunities, setting clear expectations, showing up and being reliable, and reflecting on your experience, you can volunteer effectively. Additionally, it's important to be flexible, follow-up, and give back in different ways.

Can I make a difference with a small donation?

Many people believe that their donation is too small to make a difference, but this is not necessarily the case. While large donations may have a greater immediate impact, small donations can also make a significant difference, especially when they are combined with the donations of many others.

One of the main advantages of small donations is that they can be an accessible way for people to get involved in philanthropy and engage with causes they care about. This can be especially important for people who may not have a lot of resources, but still want to make a positive impact on the world.

Small donations can also be an effective way to support grassroots organizations and causes that may not have the resources to attract large donations. These organizations often rely on the support of many small donors to sustain their work, and small donations can be a vital source of funding for them.

Another advantage of small donations is that they can be used to make a difference in a variety of ways. For example, small donations can be used to support specific programs or projects, such as building a school or providing clean water to a community. They can also be used to support general operations, such as staffing or administrative costs.

Additionally, small donations can also be bundled with other small donations, through platforms like crowd-funding, which can create a significant impact.

It's also worth noting that small donations can be a stepping stone to more significant philanthropy. By making small donations, people can learn more about the causes they care about, and this can help them make more informed decisions about their giving in the future.

In conclusion, small donations can make a meaningful difference, especially when they are combined with the donations of many others.

They can be an accessible way for people to get involved in philanthropy, support grassroots organizations and causes, and make a difference in a variety of ways. Additionally, small donations can be a stepping stone to more significant philanthropy. It's important to remember that every little bit counts and that any donation, no matter how small, can make an impact.

Example of how to create a philanthropic mindset with a salary of $100,000 per year:

Creating a philanthropic mindset with a salary of $100,000 per year is an achievable goal that can make a significant difference in the world. Here's an example of how you can create a philanthropic mindset with a salary of $100,000 per year:

1. **Identify your values and passions:** Start by thinking about the issues and causes that align with your values and passions. For example, you may care deeply about environmental conservation, education, or healthcare.

2. **Research potential causes and organizations:** Once you have identified your values and passions, research different causes and organizations that align with them. Look for information on the organization's mission, impact, and financial stability.

3. **Assess your resources:** Consider how much time, money, and other resources you have available to give. Based on your $100,000 salary, you may decide to allocate a certain percentage of your income to philanthropy each year. For example, you could commit to giving away 10% of your salary or $10,000 per year.

4. **Create a budget:** Create a budget for your giving that includes both short-term and long-term goals. Be realistic about what you can afford to give while also considering your long-term financial plans.

5. **Set clear and measurable goals:** Set specific, measurable goals for your giving. For example, you may want to support a specific organization or cause, and want to track the impact of your donation over time.

6. **Be flexible and adaptable:** Be prepared to make adjustments to your plan as you learn more about the organizations and causes you support. Be open to new opportunities and be willing to re-evaluate your goals and priorities as needed.

By following these steps, you can create a philanthropic mindset that aligns with your values, passions, and resources. Remember to keep an open mind and be flexible as you navigate through your philanthropic journey. Additionally, you can also seek advice from a financial advisor to help you make a plan that fits your overall financial goals.

Setting financial goals and creating a plan to achieve them

Setting financial goals for giving is an important step in creating a philanthropic plan. Here are the steps you can take to set financial goals for giving and create a plan to achieve them:

1. **Determine your giving budget:** Start by assessing your current financial situation and determining how much you can realistically afford to give. Consider factors such as your income, expenses, and long-term financial goals.

2. **Set a specific giving percentage or dollar amount:** Decide on a specific percentage or dollar amount that you want to give each year. This can be a percentage of your income or a specific dollar amount. For example, you may decide to give away 10% of your income or $50,000 per year.

3. **Create a budget for your giving:** Once you have determined your giving budget, create a budget for your giving that includes both short-term and long-term goals. Be realistic about what you can afford to give while also considering your long-term financial plans.

4. **Set clear and measurable goals:** Set specific, measurable goals for your giving. For example, you may want to support a

specific organization or cause, and want to track the impact of your donation over time.

5. **Create a giving plan:** Use your budget and goals to create a giving plan that outlines how you will allocate your giving budget. This plan should include the organizations and causes you want to support, the amount you want to give, and the timing of your donations.

6. **Review and adjust your plan regularly:** Review your giving plan regularly, and make adjustments as necessary. Be open to new opportunities and be willing to re-evaluate your goals and priorities as needed.

By following these steps, you can set financial goals for giving and create a plan to achieve them. Remember that setting financial goals for giving and creating a plan to achieve them, is an ongoing process and should be reviewed and adjusted as your financial situation changes.

Top financial goals for wealthy people who want to give back

Do any of these sound familiar? Wealthy individuals have the opportunity to make a significant impact through their giving, and setting financial goals for philanthropy is an important step in creating a meaningful and impactful giving plan. Here are some top financial goals for wealthy individuals who want to give back:

1. **Create a charitable trust or foundation:** Creating a charitable trust or foundation can be an effective way for wealthy individuals to make a long-term impact through their giving. These vehicles can provide tax benefits, and allow you to make a significant impact over the long term.

2. **Invest in impactful causes:** Impact investing is a way for wealthy individuals to use their resources to generate

measurable, beneficial social or environmental impact alongside a financial return. This can be a way to make a difference while also achieving financial returns.

3. **Make a major gift:** Making a major gift to an organization or cause can have a significant impact and can also be a way to leave a lasting legacy.

4. **Get involved in philanthropic leadership:** Wealthy individuals can take on leadership roles in philanthropy by serving on boards, joining giving circles, and participating in philanthropic networks. This can be a way to make a difference while also gaining valuable insights and connections.

5. **Encourage others to give**: Wealthy individuals can also encourage others to give by setting an example, mentoring others, and supporting initiatives that promote philanthropy.

By setting financial goals for giving, wealthy individuals can make a significant impact on the world while also achieving their own personal and professional goals. Remember, that setting financial goals for giving is an ongoing process, and should be reviewed and adjusted as your financial situation changes.

World's Wealthiest Philanthropists and How They Became Wealthy

Bill Gates - Co-founder of Microsoft and one of the wealthiest people in the world, Bill Gates became wealthy through his success in the technology industry. He and his wife Melinda founded the Bill and Melinda Gates Foundation, which focuses on improving healthcare and reducing poverty around the world.

Warren Buffett - One of the most successful investors in history, Warren Buffett became wealthy through his investments in companies such as Berkshire Hathaway. He has pledged to give away the majority of his fortune through the Giving Pledge, which encourages billionaires to give away at least half of their wealth to philanthropy.

Mark Zuckerberg - Co-founder and CEO of Facebook, Mark Zuckerberg became wealthy through the success of the social media platform. He and his wife Priscilla Chan founded the Chan Zuckerberg Initiative, which focuses on education, healthcare, and science.

Larry Ellison - Co-founder and former CEO of Oracle, Larry Ellison became wealthy through the success of the technology company. He has given significant donations to medical research, education, and the arts.

Larry Page - Co-founder of Google and one of the wealthiest people in the world, Larry Page became wealthy through the success of the search engine company. He has made significant donations to a variety of causes through the Carl Victor Page Memorial Foundation, which focuses on technology and scientific research.

Sergey Brin - Co-founder of Google and one of the wealthiest people in the world, Sergey Brin became wealthy through the success of the search engine company. He has made significant donations to a variety of causes through the Brin Wojcicki Foundation, which focuses on science, technology, and education.

Elon Musk - Founder of SpaceX and Tesla, Elon Musk became wealthy through his success in the technology and energy industries. He has made significant donations to a variety of causes, including education, science, and renewable energy.

Oprah Winfrey - One of the most successful television personalities in history, Oprah Winfrey became wealthy through her talk show and media empire. She has made significant donations to education, healthcare, and the arts through the Oprah Winfrey Charitable Foundation.

Michael Bloomberg - Founder of Bloomberg LP, a financial data and media company, and former Mayor of New York City, Michael Bloomberg became wealthy through his successful business ventures. He has made significant donations to a variety of causes through the Bloomberg Philanthropies.

Richard Branson - Founder of the Virgin Group, which includes a variety of companies in industries such as transportation, healthcare, and entertainment, Richard Branson became wealthy through his business ventures. He has made significant donations to a variety of causes through the Virgin Unite, which focuses on entrepreneurship, education, and the environment.

It's worth noting that, many of these philanthropists have also been successful entrepreneurs and have made their fortunes through their own business

CHAPTER 2

Identifying Your Values & Budget

Identifying your values is an essential step in creating a plan for philanthropy. When you align your values with your giving, you can ensure that your resources are being directed towards causes and organizations that align with what you care about most deeply. This can increase the impact of your giving and make your philanthropy more meaningful and fulfilling.

Here are 15 values that many philanthropists have:

1. **Altruism:** A desire to help others and make a positive impact in the world.

2. **Empathy:** The ability to understand and share the feelings of others.

3. **Compassion:** A deep awareness of the suffering of others and a desire to alleviate it.

4. **Justice:** A belief in fairness and equality for all.

5. **Human rights:** A belief in the inherent dignity and worth of every person.

6. **Environmentalism:** A concern for the health and well-being of the planet and its inhabitants.

7. **Education:** A belief in the importance of education and the role it plays in creating a better world.

8. **Health:** A belief in the importance of access to quality healthcare for all.

9. **Economic development:** A belief in the importance of economic growth and stability for individuals and communities.

10. **Community:** A belief in the importance of building strong, supportive communities.

11. **Diversity and inclusion:** A belief in the importance of respecting and valuing diversity and inclusivity.

12. **Creativity:** A belief in the power of creativity to make a positive impact in the world.

13. **Innovation:** A belief in the power of new ideas and technologies to create positive change.

14. **Philanthropy:** A belief in the importance of giving back to others and making a difference in the world.

15. **Sustainability:** A belief in the importance of preserving natural resources and creating a sustainable future for all.

By identifying your values, you can ensure that your giving aligns with what you care about most deeply and make a more meaningful and impactful difference in the world. Remember, that these values are not mutually exclusive, and a philanthropist may identify with several values at the same time. It's also important to note that these values may change and evolve over time, and it's important to keep re-evaluating them.

There are various types of philanthropic investments that individuals can make to grow their wealth, including:

There are several types of philanthropic investments that individuals can make to grow their wealth. Here are some examples:

1. **Impact investing:** This type of investment involves investing in companies, funds, or projects that have a measurable

positive social or environmental impact. This can include investments in renewable energy, sustainable agriculture, or affordable housing.

2. **Community investing:** This type of investment involves investing in organizations or projects that benefit low-income or underserved communities. This can include investments in microfinance, community development, or affordable housing.

3. **Philanthropic real estate**: This type of investment involves purchasing property or investing in real estate developments that have a social or environmental impact. This can include investments in affordable housing, green buildings, or community development projects.

4. **Social enterprise:** This type of investment involves investing in businesses that have a social or environmental mission. This can include investments in companies that produce sustainable products, provide job training for disadvantaged individuals, or operate in under-served markets.

5. **Program-related investments (PRIs):** This type of investment is offered by foundations and allows them to invest in organizations or projects that align with their mission. PRIs can take the form of loans, guarantees, or equity investments.

6. **Mission-related investments (MRIs):** This type of investment is offered by endowments, foundations, and other philanthropic organizations, and is made to generate a financial return while aligning with the mission of the organization.

7. **Donor-advised funds (DAFs)**: These are charitable giving vehicles that allow donors to make a charitable contribution,

receive an immediate tax benefit, and then recommend grants to charitable organizations over time.

8. **Carbon offsetting:** This type of investment involves investing in projects or initiatives that reduce carbon emissions.

These are just a few examples of the various types of philanthropic investments that individuals can make to grow their wealth. It's important to note that these investments come with different levels of risk and return.

The returns on philanthropic investments can vary widely depending on the specific investment and the market conditions at the time. Some investments may generate higher returns than others, but it's important to remember that the primary goal of philanthropic investing is not necessarily to generate the highest possible returns, but to create a positive social or environmental impact while also generating a financial return.

That being said, Impact investing is considered as one of the most common types of philanthropic investment for the highest returns. Impact investing is becoming an increasingly popular way for individuals to align their values with their investments, and the returns on impact investments can be competitive with traditional investments. Impact investments can be made in a variety of sectors such as renewable energy, sustainable agriculture, or affordable housing and can generate positive social or environmental impact.

It's also important to note that returns on philanthropic investments can be difficult to predict, and some investments may not generate any return at all. Therefore, it's important to consult with a financial advisor and/or a professional in the field before making any investments.

Methods wealthy people use to earn passive income out of Philanthropy:

There are several ways in which wealthy individuals can use philanthropy to earn passive income. Here are some examples:

1. **Philanthropic real estate:** Investing in properties or real estate developments that have a social or environmental impact, such as affordable housing or green buildings, can generate rental income or capital appreciation. **<u>This is considered one of the steadiest.</u>**

2. **Social impact bonds (SIBs):** These are financial instruments that allow investors to provide capital to social service programs in exchange for a return if the program achieves certain milestones.

3. **Community investing:** Investing in organizations or projects that benefit low-income or underserved communities can generate a financial return through interest or dividends. **<u>This is considered one of the steadiest.</u>**

4. **Mission-related investments (MRIs):** Investing in companies, funds, or projects that align with a philanthropic mission can generate returns through dividends, capital appreciation, or interest. **<u>This is considered one of the steadiest.</u>**

5. **Carbon offsetting:** Investing in projects or initiatives that reduce carbon emissions can generate returns through the sale of carbon credits.**<u>This is considered one of the steadiest.</u>**

6. **Program-related investments (PRIs):** Foundations can make investments in organizations or projects that align with their mission and earn a return on their investment.

7. **Donor-advised funds (DAFs):** DAFs allow donors to make a charitable contribution and then recommend grants to

charitable organizations over time. The contributions made to the DAFs can be invested, which can generate a return over time. **This is considered one of the steadiest.**

8. **Community Development Financial Institutions (CDFIs):** Investing in CDFIs can be a way to generate a return while also supporting economic development in low-income communities.**This is considered one of the steadiest.**

9. **Community Land Trusts**: Investing in Community Land Trusts, a non-profit organization that acquires and holds land for the benefit of a community, can generate rental income from the properties.

10. **Philanthropic lending:** Investing in organizations that provide loans to under-served communities, such as microfinance institutions, can generate returns through interest.**This is considered one of the steadiest.**

11. **Social impact funds:** Investing in funds that focus on companies or projects with a positive social or environmental impact can generate returns through dividends, capital appreciation, or interest.

12. **Crowdfunding:** Investing in crowdfunding campaigns that support social or environmental causes can generate returns through rewards or equity in the project.

13. **Community shares:** Investing in community shares, which are offered by community-based organizations, can generate returns through dividends or capital appreciation. **This is considered one of the steadiest.**

14. **Socially Responsible Investing (SRI) funds:** Investing in SRI funds, which are focused on companies that adhere to certain environmental, social and governance standards, can

generate returns through dividends, capital appreciation, or interest.**This is considered one of the steadiest.**

15. **Philanthropic venture capital:** Investing in venture capital funds that focus on companies or projects with a positive social or environmental impact can generate returns through equity in the company.

16. **Philanthropic annuities:** Investing in annuities that support charitable causes, can generate returns through regular payments over a period of time.

17. **Philanthropic leasing:** Investing in leasing companies that provide equipment or vehicles to organizations that support social or environmental causes can generate returns through rental income.

18. **Philanthropic royalties:** Investing in companies or projects that generate royalties from the sale of products or services that support social or environmental causes can generate returns through royalties payments.

19. **Green Bonds:** Investing in bonds that are issued to support environmentally friendly projects such as renewable energy, can generate returns through interest payments.

20. **Community banks:** Investing in community banks, which are locally-owned and -controlled, can generate returns through interest or dividends and can also benefit the community.

21. **Community foundations:** Investing in community foundations, which are philanthropic organizations that support local causes, can generate returns through dividends, capital appreciation, or interest.

22. **Philanthropic mutual funds:** Investing in mutual funds that focus on companies or projects with a positive social or

environmental impact can generate returns through dividends, capital appreciation, or interest.

23. **Community share:** Investing in community shares, which are offered by community-based organizations, can generate returns through dividends or capital appreciation.

It's important to note that returns on philanthropic investments can be difficult to predict, and some investments may not generate any return at all. Additionally, in some cases, the primary goal of philanthropy may not be to earn passive income, but to make a positive impact on the world. Therefore, it's important to consult with a financial advisor and/or a professional in the field before making any investments, and to be aware of the associated risks.

Using Asset Allocation and Diversification of Investments to Build Wealth

How do I determine where to give my charitable donations? Asset allocation and diversification of investments are important strategies for giving back and achieving philanthropic goals. By allocating assets across different types of investments, individuals can balance risk and return, while also aligning their investments with their values and philanthropic goals.

Asset allocation is the process of dividing an investment portfolio among different asset categories, such as stocks, bonds, and cash. The idea behind asset allocation is to spread risk among different types of investments, so that a loss in one category can be offset by gains in another. This can help to reduce overall portfolio volatility and increase the likelihood of achieving long-term investment goals.

Diversification is the process of spreading investments across different asset classes, sectors, and geographies. Diversification can help to reduce the risk of concentrated investments in a single company or industry. By spreading investments across different asset classes, sectors, and geographies, investors can reduce the impact of market fluctuations and increase the chances of achieving their long-term investment goals.

When it comes to philanthropy, asset allocation and diversification can be used to align investments with values and philanthropic goals. For example, an individual may choose to allocate a portion of their portfolio to impact investments, such as renewable energy, sustainable agriculture, or affordable housing, in order to generate a financial return while also making a positive impact on the world.

In addition, many individuals use diversification strategies to invest in community development financial institutions (CDFIs), microfinance institutions, community land trusts, and other organizations that support under-served communities. This can generate a financial return while also supporting economic development in low-income communities.

Another way to diversify and align investments with philanthropic goals is to invest in socially responsible investment (SRI) funds or mission-related investments (MRIs). These funds invest in companies that align with certain environmental, social, and governance standards. This can generate a financial return while also supporting causes that align with personal values.

Is it better to give to large, well-established organizations or smaller, local charities?

The question of whether it is better to give to large, well-established organizations or smaller, local charities is a complex one that depends on a variety of factors, including the philanthropist's goals, values, and resources.

One of the main advantages of giving to large, well-established organizations is that they often have more resources and expertise to tackle complex social and environmental issues. They may also have more established track records and be able to demonstrate a clear impact and outcomes achieved. Additionally, many large organizations are well-regarded, and have a good reputation, which can be an important factor for donors who want to ensure that their money is being used effectively.

On the other hand, small, local charities may be more nimble and able to respond quickly to changing needs in their communities. They may also be better connected to the people they serve and have a deeper understanding of the specific challenges faced by the community. Additionally, giving to local charities can have a more immediate and visible impact on the community and can help to build a sense of connection and engagement with the causes that philanthropists care about.

However, it's worth noting that both large and small organizations have their own strengths and challenges. Additionally, both types of organizations can have a positive impact on the community and address certain issues. Therefore, it's important to conduct due diligence and research organizations before making a donation, regardless of their size.

Additionally, many philanthropists choose to give to both large and small organizations, as part of a diversified philanthropy strategy. This can allow them to support causes and organizations that align with their values and interests, while also ensuring that their giving is having a meaningful impact.

Another important factor to consider is the alignment of the philanthropist's values, goals and giving strategy with the organization. This can be done by researching the organizations' mission, goals, programs and impact, as well as by speaking with staff, volunteers, and beneficiaries of the organization.

CHAPTER 3

How to Assess Impact of Your Giving

Assessing the impact of your giving is an important step in ensuring that your philanthropy is making a meaningful difference in the world. By measuring the impact of your giving, you can make informed decisions about where to focus your resources and make adjustments as needed to maximize your impact.

One way to assess the impact of your giving is through outcome evaluation. This approach measures the results of a particular program or project, such as the number of people served or the specific outcomes achieved. This can be done through surveys, focus groups, or other data collection methods. Outcome evaluations can help you understand whether a program or project is achieving its intended goals and identify areas for improvement.

Another approach is process evaluation, which looks at how a program or project is implemented. This can include things like the quality of staff training, the level of participant engagement, and the overall program design. Process evaluations can help you identify any issues with implementation that may be impacting the success of a program or project.

Impact evaluations are another way of assessing the impact of your giving, which aims to measure the overall impact of a program or project on a certain population or community, as well as the underlying causes of this impact. This can be done through randomized control trials, quasi-experimental designs, and other methods. Impact evaluations can help you understand the broader impact of your giving and identify areas where additional resources may be needed.

You can also use a combination of these methods to assess the impact of your giving. For example, you may use outcome evaluation to measure the results of a program, and process evaluation to understand how the program is implemented.

Another way to assess the impact of your giving is through benchmarking. This involves comparing the performance of a program or project to that of similar programs or projects in the same field. Benchmarking can help you understand how your program or project stacks up against others in terms of effectiveness and efficiency.

Additionally, it is important to consider the perspectives of the beneficiaries of your giving, as they can provide valuable insights into the impact of your giving. This can be done through feedback forms, interviews, and focus groups.

Finally, it is important to regularly review and update your giving strategy based on the results of your impact assessments. This can involve reallocating resources, adjusting program design, or identifying new opportunities for giving.

Assessing the impact of your giving is an ongoing process that requires regular monitoring, data collection, and analysis. By taking the time to evaluate the impact of your giving, you can ensure that your philanthropy is making a meaningful difference in the world and make adjustments as needed to maximize your impact.

How to Understand and Evaluate Different Philanthropic Investment Vehicles

When it comes to philanthropy, there are a wide variety of investment vehicles available to individuals who want to give back and achieve their philanthropic goals. Understanding and evaluating different philanthropic investment vehicles can help ensure that your resources are directed towards causes and organizations that align with what you care about most deeply.

One way to understand and evaluate different philanthropic investment vehicles is to consider their potential impact. **For example, impact investments, such as renewable energy, sustainable agriculture, or affordable housing, can have a measurable positive social or environmental impact**. Community investing, such as microfinance, community development, or affordable housing, can benefit low-income or underserved communities. Philanthropic real estate, such as affordable housing or green buildings, can have a positive impact on the environment and the community.

Another way to evaluate different philanthropic investment vehicles is to consider their financial returns. Some philanthropic investment vehicles, such as impact investments or community investing, may generate a financial return that is similar to traditional investments. Other investment vehicles, such as program-related investments (PRIs) or philanthropic real estate, may generate a lower financial return but may also have a greater potential impact.

Additionally, it's important to consider the level of risk associated with different philanthropic investment vehicles. Some investments may be considered higher risk, such as impact investments or community investing, while others may be considered lower risk, such as philanthropic real estate or program-related investments (PRIs).

It's also important to consider the alignment of philanthropic investment vehicles with your personal values and philanthropic goals. For example, if you are particularly passionate about environmental causes, you may want to consider investing in impact investments that focus on renewable energy or sustainable agriculture.

It's important to note that philanthropic investment vehicles come with different levels of risk and returns, and it's important to consult with a financial advisor and/or a professional in the field before making any investments. It's also important to remember that these investments are not mutually exclusive and a philanthropist may invest in several vehicles at the same time. It's also important to note that these investments may change and evolve over time, and it's important to keep re-evaluating them.

Sample of a $1,000,000 Impactful Investment Plan

An impactful philanthropic investment with $1,000,000 over 5 years could take many forms, depending on the philanthropist's goals and values. Here is an example of one possible scenario: The philanthropist has a strong interest in addressing poverty and increasing access to education in developing countries. They decide to invest $1,000,000 over 5 years in a nonprofit organization that works to build schools and provide education opportunities for children living in poverty in sub-Saharan Africa.

The organization has a track record of successfully building schools and providing education opportunities in the region, and has a detailed plan for how they will use the $1,000,000 investment. They plan to use the funds to construct 10 new schools in rural areas, each serving 300 children. They will also provide teacher training, educational materials, and other resources to ensure that the schools are effective and sustainable.

The philanthropist works closely with the organization to track the progress of the investment and assess the impact of their giving. They conduct regular site visits to the schools, collect data on student enrollment and performance, and gather feedback from parents and community members.

After 5 years, the philanthropist is able to see the tangible impact of their investment. The 10 new schools have been constructed, and more than 3,000 children are now able to access education opportunities that they would not have otherwise had. The schools have improved the children's academic performance, and the students are now more likely to continue their education and have more opportunities in the future.

Additionally, the philanthropist has noticed a positive impact on the communities where the schools were built. With more children going to school, parents have more time to work, which helps to improve the economic situation of the communities. The organization also provided a source of income for local people as they were hired to build the schools.

This example is just one of many ways that a philanthropist could invest $1,000,000 over 5 years to make a meaningful impact. The most important thing is to align the investment with the philanthropist's goals, values, and interests and to have a clear plan for how the funds will be used and how the impact will be measured.

How to Measure the Effectiveness of Charitable Organizations

Measuring the effectiveness of charitable organizations is an important step in ensuring that your philanthropy is making a meaningful difference in the world. Here are some steps you can take to measure the effectiveness of charitable organizations:

Define your goals and objectives: Before you can measure the effectiveness of a charitable organization, you need to have a clear understanding of what you hope to achieve through your giving. This will help you identify the specific outcomes and impact you want to measure.

Research the organization: Before you make a donation, it's important to research the organization and their programs to understand their mission, goals, and track record. This can include looking at their website, financial statements, and annual reports, as well as speaking with staff, volunteers, and beneficiaries of the organization.

Identify the right metrics: Once you have a clear understanding of the organization and your goals, you need to identify the metrics that will be most meaningful in measuring the effectiveness of the organization. These metrics should be specific, measurable, and relevant to the organization's mission and your goals.

Collect data: Once you have identified the metrics, you need to collect data on the organization's performance. This can include things like the number of people served, the outcomes achieved, and the cost per outcome.

Analyze the data: After you have collected the data, it's important to analyze it to understand the organization's performance. This can include comparing the organization's performance to that of similar organizations, or looking for patterns or trends in the data over time.

Communicate with the organization: After you have analyzed the data, it's important to communicate with the organization about your findings. Share your analysis with the organization and ask for their perspective on the data and insights. This can help you gain a deeper understanding of the organization's performance and identify areas for improvement.

Use the data to make decisions: Once you have analyzed the data and communicated with the organization, use the information to make decisions about your giving. This can include reallocating resources, adjusting your giving strategy, or identifying new opportunities for giving.

Repeat the process: Measuring the effectiveness of charitable organizations is an ongoing process. It's important to repeat the process regularly, updating your goals and objectives as needed, and continuing to collect and analyze data on the organization's performance.

Share your findings: Share your findings with others in your network, such as family members, friends and other donors. Sharing your findings can help others make informed decisions about their own giving and it can also help to increase transparency and accountability in the nonprofit sector.

Reflect on your philanthropy: Take time to reflect on your philanthropy and how it aligns with your values and goals. Use the information you've gathered to make adjustments as needed and continue to evolve your giving over time.

It's worth noting that measuring the effectiveness of charitable organizations can be challenging and there is no one-size-fits-all approach. It's important to be realistic about what can be achieved and to be open to learning and adjusting your approach as needed. Additionally, it's recommended to always consult with a professional advisor or expert before making any significant philanthropic decisions.

CHAPTER 4

Top Giving Strategies of the Wealthy

Wealthy individuals use different strategies to maximize their giving because it allows them to align their philanthropy with their values and interests, achieve their philanthropic goals, and maximize the impact of their giving. Different giving strategies offer different benefits and limitations. For example, direct giving allows for quick and easy donations to a specific cause, while philanthropic trusts allow for donations over time. Impact investing allows for the potential for both a financial and social return, but it also carries investment risks.

Private foundations offer more control over the distribution of funds, but also require significant resources to set up and maintain. Donor-advised funds provide a flexible giving option, but with less control over the final distribution of funds. By using a combination of strategies, wealthy individuals can create a diversified philanthropic portfolio that meets their specific needs, values, and goals. Additionally, many wealthy individuals seek professional advice from philanthropy consultants or experts to help them identify the most effective giving strategies and maximize their impact.

60 Investment Strategies That are Commonly Used By The Wealthy

1. **Direct giving:** Donating money directly to charitable organizations or causes.

2. **Philanthropic trusts:** Setting up a trust to make charitable donations over time.

3. **Impact investing**: Investing in companies, funds, or projects that have a social or environmental impact.

4. **Private foundations**: Establishing a private foundation to manage philanthropic giving.

5. **Donor-advised funds**: Making a charitable contribution to a fund that can be distributed to different organizations over time.

6. **Socially responsible investing**: Screening investments based on social or environmental criteria.

7. **Volunteerism:** Volunteering time and skills to charitable causes.

8. **Pro bono work:** Providing professional services to non-profit organizations for free.

9. **Philanthropic consulting:** Working with a professional advisor to develop a philanthropic strategy.

10. **Community foundations:** Supporting a specific geographic area through charitable giving

11. **Charitable remainder trusts:** Providing income to the grantor during their lifetime and then distributing the remaining assets to a charity after their death.

12. **Charitable lead trusts:** Providing income to a charity for a set period of time and then distributing the remaining assets to the grantor or their heirs.

13. **Program-related investments:** Investing in organizations or projects that align with the foundation's mission, with the expectation of a financial return.

14. **Mission-related investments:** Investing in companies, funds, or projects that align with the foundation's mission, without the expectation of a financial return.

15. **Philanthropic real estate:** Donating or investing in real estate for the benefit of charitable causes.

16. **Philanthropic travel:** Combining travel with volunteerism or philanthropy.

17. **Employee giving programs:** Encouraging employees to donate money or time to charitable causes, often through payroll deductions.

18. **Cause-related marketing:** Partnering with a business to promote a charitable cause and donate a portion of the proceeds.

19. **Fundraising events:** Hosting fundraising events to raise money for charitable causes.

20. **Philanthropic legacy planning:** Incorporating charitable giving into estate planning to ensure that assets are distributed to charitable causes after death.

21. **Philanthropic capital campaigns:** Raising large sums of money for a specific charitable project or organization.

22. **Philanthropic capital pools:** Pooling funds from multiple donors to make larger impactful investments or grants.

23. **Philanthropic incubation:** Providing resources and support to organizations and projects in their early stages to help them become self-sustaining.

24. **Philanthropic intermediaries:** Organizations that facilitate philanthropic giving by connecting donors with causes and organizations in need of funding.

25. **Philanthropic networks:** Groups of individuals or organizations that come together to pool resources and work towards a common philanthropic goal.

26. **Philanthropic sector investing:** Investing in companies that are focused on the creation of social and environmental impact, also known as "impact companies"

27. **Philanthropic education:** Providing education and training to individuals and organizations on effective philanthropic strategies and practices.

28. **Philanthropic capital aggregation:** Pooling resources from multiple donors to increase the effectiveness of a specific philanthropic project or organization.

29. **Philanthropic bundling:** Combining multiple forms of philanthropy, such as volunteering, pro bono work, and financial contributions, to maximize impact.

30. **Philanthropic mentoring:** Providing guidance and advice to individuals or organizations on effective philanthropic strategies and practices.

31. **Philanthropic collaboration:** Working with other organizations or individuals to achieve a common philanthropic goal.

32. **Philanthropic partnerships:** Forming long-term partnerships between philanthropic organizations and other organizations or individuals to achieve a shared mission.

33. **Philanthropic consulting:** Working with professional advisors to develop a comprehensive and effective philanthropic strategy.

34. **Philanthropic technology:** Using technology to improve the effectiveness of philanthropic efforts, such as online donation platforms or impact measurement tools.

35. **Philanthropic research:** Conducting research to identify the most effective philanthropic strategies and practices.

36. **Philanthropic matching:** Encouraging philanthropic giving by matching donations from individuals or organizations.

37. **Philanthropic storytelling:** Using storytelling to raise awareness and support for charitable causes.

38. **Philanthropic storytelling:** Using storytelling to raise awareness and support for charitable causes.

39. **Philanthropy-related tax incentives:** Taking advantage of tax incentives for charitable giving.

40. **Philanthropic co-creation:** Involving beneficiaries in the design, implementation and evaluation of philanthropy projects

41. **Philanthropic crowdfunding:** Raising funds for a charitable cause through online platforms that allow individuals to make small contributions.

42. **Philanthropic endowment:** Setting up a fund that is invested and the income is used to support charitable causes over time.

43. **Philanthropic venture capital:** Investing in early-stage companies that have a social or environmental impact.

44. **Philanthropic debt financing:** Providing loans or other forms of debt financing to organizations or projects that have a social or environmental impact.

45. **Philanthropic equity financing:** Investing in companies or organizations by purchasing shares of stock.

46. **Philanthropic leasing:** Leasing property, equipment or other assets to organizations or projects that have a social or environmental impact.

47. **Philanthropic leasing:** Leasing property, equipment or other assets to organizations or projects that have a social or environmental impact.

48. **Philanthropic consulting:** Providing advice and support to individuals or organizations on how to be more effective in their philanthropic efforts.

49. **Philanthropic events:** Organizing or participating in events such as galas, auctions, or charity runs to raise money for charitable causes.

50. **Philanthropic challenges:** Encouraging philanthropy by issuing challenges to individuals or organizations to give a certain amount of money or time to a charitable cause.

51. **Philanthropic auction:** Organizing or participating in auctions where proceeds go towards charitable causes.

52. **Philanthropic sports:** Organizing or participating in sports events where proceeds go towards charitable causes.

53. **Philanthropic art:** Organizing or participating in art exhibitions, auctions or other events where proceeds go towards charitable causes.

54. **Philanthropic gaming:** Organizing or participating in gaming events where proceeds go towards charitable causes.

55. **Philanthropic prize:** Offering a prize or awards to individuals or organizations that achieve a certain level of philanthropic impact.

56. **Philanthropic incubation:** Providing resources and support to new or struggling philanthropic organizations to help them become sustainable.

57. **Philanthropic co-creation:** Involving beneficiaries in designing, implementing and evaluating philanthropy projects

58. **Philanthropic public-private partnership**: Collaborating with public sector organizations to achieve shared philanthropic goals.

59. **Philanthropic social enterprise:** Starting a business that aims to generate a social or environmental impact along with a financial return.

60. **Philanthropic storytelling:** Utilizing storytelling to inspire and mobilize people around a certain cause or organization.

Getting Your Business Involved in Philanthropy

Corporate social responsibility (CSR) and cause marketing are two important concepts that have become increasingly relevant in today's business world. Both CSR and cause marketing involve companies taking steps to improve the social and environmental impact of their operations, and to support causes and organizations that align with their values and mission.

Corporate social responsibility refers to the actions that companies take to meet the expectations of their stakeholders, including shareholders, employees, customers, and the community. This can include initiatives such as reducing environmental impact, promoting workplace diversity and inclusion, and supporting local communities. CSR is often seen as a way for companies to "give back" to society and to demonstrate their commitment to ethical and sustainable business practices.

Cause marketing is a type of marketing that involves companies partnering with non-profit organizations or causes to promote a specific message or campaign. This can include things like promoting a particular charity, raising awareness about a social issue, or encouraging customers to take action to support a cause. Cause marketing is often seen as a way for companies to build brand loyalty and connect with customers on a deeper level, while also making a positive impact on society.

One example of CSR and cause marketing in action is the partnership between a major retail company and a non-profit organization that focuses on fighting poverty. The company has committed to providing jobs and training opportunities for people living in low-income communities, and also supports the non-profit through donations and in-store promotions. This partnership not only benefits the community, but also helps the company to build a positive reputation and connect with customers who are passionate about social issues. Another example is when a company decides to stop using single use plastic and invest in alternative materials, this action not only helps the environment but also helps the company to build a reputation of being environmentally friendly and responsible.

Corporate social responsibility and cause marketing are both important ways for companies to improve their social and environmental impact and connect with customers on a deeper level. These initiatives can help companies to build a positive reputation, increase brand loyalty, and make a positive impact on society. As consumers become increasingly conscious of the impact of their purchasing decisions on the environment and society, CSR and cause marketing will likely become even more important for companies looking to succeed in today's business world.

Incorporating philanthropy into a business can have a positive impact on both the community and the company. It can improve the company's reputation, boost employee morale, and even increase customer loyalty. Here are a few ways businesses can incorporate philanthropy into their operations:

1. **Corporate Giving:** Many companies have charitable foundations or programs that make donations to nonprofit organizations. These donations can be monetary, in the form of products or services, or through employee volunteerism.

2. **Cause-Related Marketing:** This strategy involves partnering with a nonprofit organization to promote a specific cause. The company donates a portion of the proceeds from the sale of a product or service to the nonprofit organization. This can be a win-win situation for both the company and the nonprofit organization.

3. **Employee Volunteerism**: Encourage employees to volunteer their time and skills to nonprofit organizations. This not only helps the community but also helps to develop the employee's skills.

4. **Socially Responsible Investing**: Companies can also use their investments to support socially responsible causes. This can include investing in companies that prioritize environmental sustainability, employee rights, and ethical business practices.

5. **Community Engagement:** Companies can also engage with their local community through initiatives such as sponsorships, grants, or community service projects.

By incorporating philanthropy into their operations, businesses can make a positive impact on the community while also enhancing their reputation and creating a positive working environment for their employees. It's important to note that all these initiatives should align with the company's values and mission and should be communicated transparently and authentically to all stakeholders.

CHAPTER 5

The Connection Between Philanthropy and Personal Wealth

Philanthropy and personal wealth are closely connected, as individuals with significant wealth often have the resources to make a significant impact through their giving. Philanthropy allows the wealthy to put their resources to work for the greater good, addressing social and environmental issues, and making a positive impact on the world.

One of the main ways that the wealthy use their wealth for philanthropy is through charitable donations. This can take many forms, such as writing a check to a nonprofit organization, creating a philanthropic trust, or setting up a private foundation. These donations can be directed towards a specific cause or organization, or can be unrestricted, allowing the charity to use the funds where they are needed most.

Another way that the wealthy use their wealth for philanthropy is through impact investing. This is a form of investment that aims to generate a social or environmental impact, in addition to a financial return. Impact investments can take many forms, such as investing in a socially responsible mutual fund, investing in a startup that has a positive social or environmental impact, or providing a loan to a small business that is working to improve the lives of people in a low-income community.

Philanthropy can also be used as a tool for estate planning, allowing the wealthy to ensure that their assets are distributed in a way that aligns with their values and makes a positive impact on the world.

This can be done through charitable bequests, charitable trusts, or other philanthropic vehicles.

Furthermore, philanthropy can also serve as a way for the wealthy to build a legacy, leaving a lasting impact on the world long after they are gone. This is a powerful motivator for many wealthy individuals, as they want to make a difference in the world and be remembered for their contributions.

In addition to the financial benefits, philanthropy can also bring personal fulfillment and a sense of purpose to the lives of the wealthy. Many wealthy individuals find that giving back to their communities and causes they care about brings them a sense of satisfaction and meaning.

It's worth noting that the connection between philanthropy and personal wealth is not limited to the wealthy. People of all income levels can make a difference through philanthropy, regardless of the amount of wealth they have. Philanthropy is about using what resources one has, whether it's time, skills, or money, to make a positive impact on the world.

Philanthropy and personal wealth are closely connected, as the wealthy often have the resources to make a significant impact through their giving. Philanthropy allows the wealthy to put their resources to work for the greater good, addressing social and environmental issues, and making a positive impact on the world. Additionally, philanthropy can also serve as a tool for estate planning, building a legacy, and bringing personal fulfillment to the lives of the wealthy. It's important to note that philanthropy is not limited to the wealthy and people of all income levels can make a difference through philanthropy.

The Importance of Balancing Short-term and Long-term Goals in Philanthropy

Philanthropy is an important aspect of personal wealth management and can be a powerful tool for making a positive impact on the world. However, it's important to balance short-term and long-term goals in order to ensure that your philanthropy is having the greatest impact possible.

Short-term goals in philanthropy are typically focused on providing immediate relief or addressing urgent needs. This can include providing aid to communities affected by natural disasters, supporting specific programs or projects, or making one-time donations to organizations. Short-term goals can be important for addressing immediate needs and providing relief to those in crisis.

Long-term goals in philanthropy, on the other hand, focus on addressing underlying issues and creating lasting change. This can include supporting an organization's mission over several years, investing in capacity building, supporting research and advocacy efforts, and creating philanthropic endowments. Long-term goals can be important for addressing underlying issues and creating lasting change.

Balancing short-term and long-term goals in philanthropy can be challenging, but it's important to consider both types of goals in order to have the most impact. For example, providing aid to a community affected by a natural disaster is a short-term goal, but investing in disaster resilience for that community can be a long-term goal.

Additionally, balancing short-term and long-term goals can also be a way to align philanthropy with the individual's values and priorities. For example, an individual who values immediate impact and addressing urgent needs may choose to focus more on short-term goals, while an individual who values creating lasting change and addressing underlying issues may choose to focus more on long-term goals.

Here are a few examples of short-term and long-term goals in philanthropy:

Short-term goals:

- Providing immediate relief to a community affected by a natural disaster, such as donating money or supplies to help with recovery efforts.

- Supporting a specific program or project, such as funding a school-building project in a developing country.

- Making a one-time donation to an organization to support their general operations or a specific program.

Long-term goals:

- Supporting an organization's mission over several years, through multi-year funding commitments.

- Investing in the capacity building of an organization to ensure its long-term sustainability.

- Supporting research and advocacy efforts to address a long-term social or environmental issue, such as climate change or poverty.

- Creating a philanthropic endowment to fund a specific cause or organization in perpetuity.

It's worth noting that these are just a few examples, and goals in philanthropy can vary greatly depending on the individual or organization's values, resources, and priorities. Additionally, philanthropy goals should be specific, measurable, achievable, relevant and time-bound (SMART) in order to be effective.

The benefits of involving your family and community in your giving

Involving your family and community in your giving can have many benefits for both you and the causes you support. Here are some of the benefits of involving your family and community in your giving:

1. **Increased Impact:** Involving your family and community in your giving can help to increase the impact of your philanthropy. By pooling resources and working together, you can amplify your giving and make a bigger difference in the world.

2. **Shared Experience:** Philanthropy can be a more meaningful and fulfilling experience when shared with others. Involving your family and community in your giving can help to create a shared sense of purpose and can be a great way to bond and build stronger relationships.

3. **Education and learning:** Involving your family and community in your giving can be a great way to educate others about the causes you care about, and to learn more about the issues you are trying to address. It also can be a great way to teach the next generation about the importance of giving back and being socially responsible.

4. **Community Building:** Involving your family and community in your giving can help to build stronger, more connected communities. By working together to support causes and organizations, you can create a sense of shared responsibility and a stronger sense of community.

5. **Legacy Building:** Involving your family and community in your giving can help to create a legacy of philanthropy that will outlive you. It can be a great way to pass on your values

and passions to future generations, and to inspire others to give back and make a difference in the world.

6. **Collaboration and networking:** Involving your family and community in your giving can also help to create opportunities for collaboration and networking with other like-minded individuals and organizations. This can help to increase your reach and impact and open up new opportunities for giving and community-building.

It's important to note that involving your family and community in your giving does not mean giving up control over your philanthropy. It's about finding a balance between involving others in the decision-making process and still following your own values and interests. It's also important to communicate and listen to the views and opinions of the members of your family and community, in order to ensure that everyone is on the same page and that the giving aligns with everyone's values and goals.

Involving your family and community in your giving can be a great way to increase the impact of your philanthropy, create shared experiences, educate and learn, build stronger communities, create a legacy, and open up opportunities for collaboration and networking. It's a powerful way to make a difference in the world and to inspire others to do the same.

CHAPTER 6

How to Protect Your Philanthropic Investments from Taxes

Wealthy individuals often donate to charitable organizations because they want to make a positive impact on the world and support causes that align with their values and interests. Philanthropy can be a powerful tool for addressing social and environmental issues and creating lasting change.

However, it's also important for wealthy individuals to protect their gifts from taxes. This is because taxes can significantly reduce the impact of a gift and the amount of money that ultimately goes to the charitable organization. By protecting their gifts from taxes, wealthy individuals can ensure that their donations have the greatest impact possible.

One of the main ways that wealthy individuals can protect their gifts from taxes is by taking advantage of tax deductions. Tax deductions are a way for individuals to lower the amount of taxes they owe by subtracting certain expenses, such as charitable donations, from their taxable income. This can significantly reduce the amount of taxes owed on a gift, which can help to maximize the impact of the donation.

Another way that wealthy individuals can protect their gifts from taxes is by setting up charitable trusts or private foundations. These structures can provide additional tax benefits, such as allowing individuals to retain control over the distribution of funds and providing income for the individual or a beneficiary.

Additionally, setting up a donor-advised fund or charitable remainder trust can also help to protect gifts from taxes, as well as providing other benefits such as flexibility in giving, and the ability to make a significant impact on multiple causes over time.

It's worth noting that tax laws can vary depending on the country or state you are in, and it's important to consult with a tax professional or financial advisor before making any decisions to ensure that the options align with your goals and that you are following the regulations of your area.

In conclusion, wealthy individuals often donate to charitable organizations because they want to make a positive impact on the world, but also want to protect their gifts from taxes to maximize their impact. This can be done by taking advantage of tax deductions, setting up charitable trusts or private foundations, and setting up donor-advised funds or charitable remainder trusts. By protecting their gifts from taxes, wealthy individuals can ensure that their donations have the greatest impact possible and can achieve their philanthropic goals more effectively.

Additionally, setting up a philanthropic strategy and working with a financial advisor can help wealthy individuals to identify tax-efficient giving options and to achieve their philanthropic goals in a more comprehensive and strategic way. It's important to remember that tax laws and regulations can vary depending on the country or state you are in, so it's important to consult with a tax professional or financial advisor before making any decisions to ensure compliance and to maximize the impact of the donation.

Here's a few ways the wealthy save money on taxes:

1. **Charitable Deduction:** Taking a charitable deduction for donations made to qualified charitable organizations can lower the amount of taxes owed on those donations.

2. **Private Foundations:** Setting up a private foundation allows for more control over the distribution of funds and can provide additional tax benefits.

3. **Donor-Advised Funds:** Setting up a donor-advised fund allows individuals to make charitable contributions and take an immediate tax deduction, while retaining the ability to recommend grants to charitable organizations in the future.

4. **Charitable Remainder Trusts:** Setting up a charitable remainder trust allows an individual to donate assets and receive an immediate tax deduction while receiving income from those assets for a period of time.

5. **Charitable Lead Trusts:** Setting up a charitable lead trust allows an individual to donate assets and receive an immediate tax deduction while providing income to a charitable organization for a period of time.

6. **Charitable Gift Annuities:** Setting up a charitable gift annuity allows an individual to donate assets and receive an immediate tax deduction while receiving income from those assets for life.

7. **Charitable Bargain Sales:** Selling an asset to a charitable organization for less than its fair market value can provide a tax benefit for the individual.

8. **Conservation Easements:** Donating a conservation easement on property to a charitable organization can provide a tax benefit for the individual.

9. **Qualified Charitable Distributions:** Individuals who are over the age of 70.5 can make a qualified charitable distribution from their IRA to a charitable organization, which can lower the amount of taxes owed on those funds.

10. **Qualified Conservation Contributions:** An individual can make a qualified conservation contribution, which allows for an immediate tax deduction and a carryforward of any unused deductions for up to 15 years.

11. **Bargain Sales to Charitable Remainder Trusts:** An individual can sell an asset to a charitable remainder trust for less than its fair market value, which can provide a tax benefit for the individual.

12. **Charitable Pooled Income Funds:** An individual can make a charitable contribution to a charitable pooled income fund, which allows for an immediate tax deduction and a lifetime income from the fund.

13. **Charitable Real Estate:** An individual can donate real estate property to a charitable organization and receive a tax benefit.

14. **Charitable Trusts:** An individual can set up a charitable trust, which allows for a tax deduction and can provide income for the individual or a beneficiary.

15. **Life Insurance:** An individual can name a charitable organization as the beneficiary of a life insurance policy, which can provide a tax benefit for the individual.

It's worth noting that these options may have different tax implications and requirements depending on the country or state you are in. Additionally, it's important to consult with a tax professional or financial advisor before making any decisions, to ensure that the options align with your goals and that you are following the regulations of your area.

How Wealthy People Use Life Insurance to Support Charitable Causes

Life insurance can be a powerful tool for wealthy individuals to use in their philanthropic efforts. Here are a few ways that wealthy individuals can use life insurance to support charitable causes:

1. **Policy Ownership:** A wealthy individual can purchase a life insurance policy and name a charitable organization as the beneficiary. This can provide a tax benefit for the individual and allow them to make a significant gift to the organization after their death.

2. **Policy Donation:** A wealthy individual can donate an existing life insurance policy to a charitable organization. The organization can then use the death benefit to support their mission.

3. **Charitable Remainder Trusts:** A wealthy individual can set up a charitable remainder trust and name the trust as the owner and beneficiary of a life insurance policy. This can provide tax benefits for the individual and allow them to make a significant gift to the trust after their death.

4. **Charitable Lead Trusts:** A wealthy individual can set up a charitable lead trust and name the trust as the owner of a life insurance policy. The trust can then use the death benefit to make payments to a charitable organization for a certain period of time.

5. **Bargain Sale:** A wealthy individual can sell a life insurance policy to a less than its cash value, providing a tax benefit for the individual and a significant gift for the organization.

6. **Split-Interest Trusts:** A wealthy individual can set up a split-interest trust, such as a charitable remainder unitrust or charitable lead trust, and name the trust as the owner of a life insurance policy. This can provide tax benefits for the individual, and allow them to make a significant gift to the trust after their death.

7. **Premium Financing:** A wealthy individual can use a strategy called premium financing, which allows them to make a large donation to a charitable organization while still maintaining control over the policy and its cash value.

8. **Charitable Gift Annuities:** A wealthy individual can make a charitable gift annuity, which allows them to donate a life insurance policy to a charitable organization and receive a tax deduction and a lifetime income from the policy.

9. **Retained Asset Accounts:** A wealthy individual can use a retained asset account, which is a type of account where the life insurance company holds the death benefit and the policy owner can access the funds while they are alive. The policy owner can then donate the funds to a charitable organization.

10. **Life Income Agreements**: A wealthy individual can make a life income agreement, which allows them to make a charitable donation of a life insurance policy and receive an income from the policy for the rest of their life.

11. **Life Settlement:** A wealthy individual can sell an existing life insurance policy to a third party for more than its cash value and use the proceeds to make a charitable donation

12. **Life Insurance Trust**: A wealthy individual can set up a life insurance trust, which allows them to make a charitable donation of a life insurance policy, and have the trust own the policy and manage it. The trust can then use the death benefit to support the charitable causes of the individual's choice.

13. **Charitable Trusts:** A wealthy individual can set up a charitable trust and name it as the beneficiary of a life insurance policy. This can provide a tax benefit for the individual and allow them to make a significant gift to the trust after their death.

14. **Policy Split:** A wealthy individual can split a life insurance policy between multiple beneficiaries, including charitable organizations, in order to distribute their wealth in an efficient manner.

15. **Policy Transfer:** A wealthy individual can transfer the ownership of a life insurance policy to a charitable organization, which can provide a tax benefit for the individual and allow them to make a significant gift to the organization.

16. **Premium-Paid Policies:** A wealthy individual can purchase a premium-paid policy, which allows them to make a charitable donation of a life insurance policy and receive a tax deduction for the premium payments.

17. **Life Insurance as Collateral:** A wealthy individual can use a life insurance policy as collateral for a loan and use the proceeds to make a charitable donation.

Which Life Insurance Policies Generate Income?

Here are the top 10 life insurance policies that generate income:

1. **Whole Life Insurance:** Whole life insurance policies offer guaranteed level premiums and cash value accumulation, which can be used as a source of income during retirement.

2. **Universal Life Insurance:** Universal life insurance policies offer flexible premiums and adjustable death benefits, which can be used as a source of income during retirement.

3. **Variable Life Insurance:** Variable life insurance policies offer cash value accumulation that is tied to the performance of underlying investments, which can be used as a source of income during retirement.

4. **Variable Universal Life Insurance**: Variable universal life insurance policies offer cash value accumulation that is tied to the performance of underlying investments and flexible premiums, which can be used as a source of income during retirement.

5. **Indexed Universal Life Insurance:** Indexed universal life insurance policies offer cash value accumulation that is tied to the performance of a stock market index and flexible premiums, which can be used as a source of income during retirement.

6. **Equity-Indexed Universal Life Insurance:** Equity-indexed universal life insurance policies offer cash value accumulation that is tied to the performance of a stock market index and flexible premiums, which can be used as a source of income during retirement.

7. **Guaranteed Universal Life Insurance:** Guaranteed universal life insurance policies offer fixed premiums and death benefits, which can be used as a source of income during retirement.

8. **Single Premium Immediate Annuity:** Single premium immediate annuity is a policy that generates a guaranteed income for a specified period of time, or for life, in exchange for a single premium payment.

9. **Deferred Annuity**: Deferred annuities are insurance policies that generate income at a later date, usually in retirement, through investments in various assets.

10. **Longevity Insurance**: Longevity insurance is a type of insurance that pays out a benefit if the insured lives to a certain age.

It's worth noting that these options may have different tax implications and requirements depending on the country or state you are in. Additionally, it's important to consult with a tax professional or financial advisor before making any decisions, to ensure that the options align with your goals and that you are following the regulations of your area.

CHAPTER 7

Using Your Platform and Influence to Promote Philanthropy

Using your platform and influence to promote philanthropy is a powerful way to make a positive impact in the world. Whether you are a business leader, public figure, or simply someone with a large social media following, you have the ability to raise awareness and inspire others to get involved in philanthropy. Here are some ways to use your platform and influence to promote philanthropy:

1. **Share your philanthropic story:** Share your personal philanthropic journey and the causes that you support. Share the impact that your giving has had and the reasons why you chose to support those causes. This will inspire others to get involved and to find causes that align with their own values and interests.

2. **Use social media:** Social media is a powerful tool for raising awareness and inspiring others to get involved in philanthropy. Share information about the causes that you support and the impact that your giving has had. Use hashtags and engage with other philanthropy advocates to expand your reach and influence.

3. **Host events and fundraisers:** Hosting events and fundraisers can be a great way to raise awareness and funds for the causes that you support. This can be a great way to engage with others and to inspire them to get involved in philanthropy.

4. **Partner with other organizations**: Partnering with other organizations can help to amplify your message and reach a wider audience. This can include working with other philanthropy advocates, businesses, or nonprofits to co-host events or to raise awareness about a specific cause.

5. **Use your platform to advocate for policy change**: You can use your platform and influence to advocate for policy change that aligns with your philanthropic goals. This can include lobbying for changes to laws or regulations that affect the causes that you support.

6. **Encourage others to give**: Use your platform and influence to encourage others to give to the causes that you support. Share information about the impact of their giving and the difference that it can make. Encourage them to research the causes and organizations they support and make informed decisions.

Using your platform and influence to promote philanthropy can have a significant impact on the world. However, it's important to be aware that with power comes responsibility. It's important to be transparent, authentic and honest in your philanthropy promotion, and to be aware that people may look up to you as an example of good practice. It's also important to acknowledge that there may be conflicts of interest, and to ensure that your philanthropy promotion is not just for self-promotion or personal gain.

By using your platform and influence to promote philanthropy, you can inspire others to get involved and make a difference in the world. It's a powerful way to create a ripple effect of positive change and to make a lasting impact on the causes and communities that you care about.

Another important aspect to consider when using your platform and influence to promote philanthropy is to be mindful of cultural sensitivity and to avoid cultural appropriation. It's important to be aware of the cultural context of the causes you support and to ensure that your philanthropy promotion is respectful and inclusive.

Additionally, it's important to be aware of the potential for exploitation, particularly when working with vulnerable communities. Make sure that your philanthropy promotion is empowering and not exploitative. It's important to work with organizations that are committed to ethical and sustainable practices and that have a deep understanding of the communities they serve.

Another important aspect to consider is to be aware of the long-term impact of your philanthropy promotion. Short-term solutions may not be sustainable in the long run. It's important to support causes and organizations that have long-term solutions and that are working to address the root causes of the problems they aim to solve.

Finally, it's important to be aware that philanthropy promotion is not a replacement for systemic change and government responsibility. While philanthropy can play an important role in addressing social issues, it should not be used as an excuse for government inaction. It's important to use your platform and influence to advocate for systemic change and to hold governments accountable for addressing social issues.

Using your platform and influence to promote philanthropy can be a powerful way to make a positive impact in the world. By being authentic, transparent, inclusive, and mindful of cultural sensitivity, and by working with trustworthy organizations, you can inspire others to get involved in philanthropy and make a real difference in the world. However, it's important to approach philanthropy promotion with responsibility and to consider the long-term impact of your giving, and to be aware of potential challenges such as cultural sensitivity, exploitation, and systemic change. By being mindful of these considerations, you can ensure that your philanthropy promotion is effective, meaningful, and truly makes a difference in the world.

Ideas for leveraging your resources, including time, money, and connections, for maximum impact.

Leveraging your resources, including time, money, and connections, is an important aspect of philanthropy. By strategically using your resources, you can maximize the impact of your giving and make a real difference in the world. Here are some ideas for leveraging your resources for maximum impact:

1. **Develop a giving plan:** Develop a giving plan that outlines your philanthropic goals and the causes that you want to support. This will help you to prioritize your giving and ensure that your resources are being used effectively to achieve your goals.

2. **Research and due diligence:** Research the organizations and causes that you want to support to ensure that they are well-managed and making a real impact. Consult charity ratings organizations, such as Charity Navigator and GuideStar, to learn more about the organization's mission, finances, and impact.

3. **Strategic and long-term giving:** Strategic and long-term giving can help you to maximize the impact of your donations and achieve your philanthropic goals more effectively. Instead of giving impulsively, take the time to research the organization and ensure that it aligns with your values and goals.

4. **Matching gifts:** Look for matching gift programs from your employer or other organizations that can double or even triple the impact of your giving.

5. **Leverage your networks and connections:** Use your networks and connections to raise awareness about the causes that you support, and to connect with other philanthropy advocates and organizations. This can help to amplify your message and reach a wider audience.

6. **Volunteer your time:** Volunteering your time can be just as valuable as giving money. Look for opportunities to volunteer with organizations that align with your values and interests, and use your skills and expertise to make a difference.

7. **Give of your professional expertise:** Consider using your professional skills and expertise to support the causes you care about. Offer pro-bono work, mentoring or consulting services, or serve on a nonprofit board, this can have a big impact on an organization's ability to achieve its mission.

8. **Consider impact investing:** Impact investing is a way to use your financial resources to support causes and organizations that align with your values, while also earning a financial return on your investment.

9. **Use your platform and influence:** Use your platform and influence to raise awareness about the causes that you support and to inspire others to get involved in philanthropy.

10. **Collaborate with others:** Collaborating with other individuals and organizations can help to amplify your impact and open up new opportunities for giving. For example, you can join a giving circle, which is a group of individuals who pool their resources and collaborate to support a specific cause or organization.

11. **Use your resources to promote systemic change:** While philanthropy can play an important role in addressing social issues, it should not be used as an excuse for government inaction. Use your resources to advocate for systemic change

and hold governments accountable for addressing social issues.

12. **Re-evaluate and adjust**: It's important to remember that your giving should be a continuous journey, and it's always good to re-evaluate and adjust your giving approach as you learn more and as the world evolves.

By leveraging your resources, including time, money, and connections, in a strategic and thoughtful way, you can maximize the impact of your giving and make a real difference in the world. It's important to remember that philanthropy is not just about the money you give, but also about the level of engagement and the impact you want to make.

It's also important to be mindful of the potential for unintended consequences and to ensure that your giving aligns with your values and goals, and that it's not causing harm to the communities you are trying to help. It's always a good practice to consult with experts and organizations that have experience and knowledge in the field, to ensure that your giving is as effective and meaningful as possible.

CHAPTER 8

Finding Trustworthy Charities to Support

Finding trustworthy charities to support is crucial for maximizing the impact of your giving and ensuring that your philanthropy is effective and meaningful. By researching and choosing a charity that is well-managed and has a track record of achieving its goals, you can be confident that your donations are making a real difference in the world. However, it's important to be aware of the potential challenges and to approach the process of finding trustworthy charities with caution and due diligence.Finding trustworthy charities to support is important for several reasons:

1. **Maximizing the impact of your giving:** Giving to a trustworthy charity ensures that your donations are being used effectively to achieve the charity's mission and make a real impact. By researching and choosing a charity that is well-managed and has a track record of achieving its goals, you can be confident that your donations are making a difference.

2. **Transparency and accountability:** Giving to a trustworthy charity means that the charity is transparent about its finances, governance, and impact. This helps to ensure that the charity is using your donations responsibly and effectively.

3. **Fulfillment and engagement:** Giving to a charity that aligns with your values and interests can be a fulfilling and meaningful experience. By choosing a charity that you are passionate about and that you feel connected to, you are more likely to be engaged with the charity over the long-term, which can lead to a more rewarding philanthropic experience.

4. **Trust and reputation:** Giving to a trustworthy charity can help to build trust and reputation. Trustworthy charities are well-respected and have a good track record of achieving their mission. This can help to build trust with donors and attract additional support.

However, finding trustworthy charities to support can also come with some challenges:

1. **Limited information:** There can be a lack of reliable information available about some charities, making it difficult to research and evaluate them.

2. **Overwhelming options:** With so many charities to choose from, it can be difficult to narrow down your search and find the right one.

3. **Limited resources:** Researching charities can be time-consuming and requires resources, such as money and expertise.

4. **Misrepresentation:** Some charities may not be completely transparent about their finances, governance, and impact, making it difficult to evaluate their trustworthiness.

Here is a process that can help you find and choose trustworthy charities to support:

1. **Identify your philanthropic goals:** Before you begin your search for charities, it's important to identify your philanthropic goals. What causes align with your values and interests? What impact do you want to make? Answering these questions will help you narrow down your search and find charities that align with your goals.

2. **Research charities:** There are a number of resources available to help you research charities. Charity ratings

organizations, such as Charity Navigator and GuideStar, provide information on a charity's finances, governance, and impact. You can also visit the charity's website to learn more about its mission, programs, and impact.

3. **Check for transparency:** A trustworthy charity should be transparent about its finances, governance, and impact. Look for a charity that makes its financial information, annual reports, and impact data readily available.

4. **Look for evidence of impact:** A trustworthy charity should be able to demonstrate the impact of its programs and activities. Look for a charity that collects and reports on data to measure its impact and evaluate its effectiveness.

5. **Consider the charity's governance:** A trustworthy charity should have strong governance practices in place. Look for a charity that has a diverse and independent board of directors, and that follows best practices for transparency and accountability.

6. **Assess the charity's reputation:** A trustworthy charity should have a good reputation within the philanthropic community. Look for a charity that is well-respected and has a good track record of achieving its mission.

7. **Make a decision:** After researching and evaluating potential charities, it's time to make a decision on which one to support. Consider which charity aligns best with your philanthropic goals and values, and which one has demonstrated a track record of effective and efficient use of resources and impact.

It's important to remember that no charity is perfect, and that choosing a charity to support is a personal decision. It's also important to remember that it's not only about the money you are giving, but also about the level of engagement and the impact you want to make.

By following this process, you can ensure that your charitable giving is effective, meaningful, and truly makes a difference in the world. It's also important to remember that your giving should be a continuous journey, and it's always good to re-evaluate and adjust your giving approach as you learn more and as the world evolves.

Emerging trends and new technologies that are shaping the field of philanthropy

There are several emerging trends and new technologies that are shaping the field of philanthropy. Here are a few examples:

1. **Social Media:** Social media platforms have become an important tool for raising awareness and inspiring others to get involved in philanthropy. Platforms like Facebook, Twitter, and Instagram have made it easy for individuals and organizations to share information and engage with others about the causes they care about.

2. **Impact Investing:** Impact investing is a way to use financial resources to support causes and organizations that align with your values, while also earning a financial return on your investment. This trend has been growing in popularity and is becoming an increasingly important way for people to align their investments with their values.

3. **Online Giving:** Online giving platforms, such as GoFundMe, Kickstarter, and Indiegogo, have made it easier for individuals and organizations to raise money for causes and projects. This has also opened up new opportunities for crowdfunding and peer-to-peer fundraising.

4. **Big Data:** Philanthropy organizations are starting to use big data to track and analyze the impact of their giving. This

allows them to make more informed decisions about where to allocate resources and how to measure the effectiveness of their programs.

5. **Blockchain:** Blockchain technology, the technology behind cryptocurrencies, has the potential to revolutionize the way that philanthropy is done, by creating transparent and secure ways to track donations and their impact.

6. **Virtual Reality:** Virtual reality technology is being used to create immersive experiences that allow donors to see the impact of their giving in a new and more engaging way.

7. **Artificial Intelligence:** AI is also being used in philanthropy, for example, to optimize donation allocation, program design and implementation, and measuring the impact of giving.

8. **Collaborative giving:** The trend of collaborative giving, where different donors pool their resources and collaborate to support a specific cause or organization, is becoming more popular.

These emerging trends and new technologies are helping to make philanthropy more efficient, effective, and engaging. They are also helping to increase transparency and accountability, and to open up new opportunities for giving and engagement. As philanthropy continues to evolve, it will be important to stay informed about these trends and to consider how they can be used to maximize the impact of your giving.

Most Commonly Donated-to Charities by the Wealthy

1. Bill and Melinda Gates Foundation

2. The Walton Family Foundation

3. The Clinton Foundation

4. The Rockefeller Foundation

5. The Ford Foundation

6. The Robert Wood Johnson Foundation

7. The W.K. Kellogg Foundation

8. The Carnegie Corporation of New York

9. The Robert and Patricia Switzer Foundation

10. The David and Lucile Packard Foundation

11. The John D. and Catherine T. MacArthur Foundation

12. The Andrew W. Mellon Foundation

13. The Open Society Foundations

14. The Annie E. Casey Foundation

15. The Gordon and Betty Moore Foundation

It's worth mentioning that these are some of the most well-known and well-established charitable foundations and organizations, but there are many other charities that also receive significant donations from wealthy individuals and philanthropic organizations.

CHAPTER 9

The Do's and Don'ts of Philanthropy

Philanthropy, or charitable giving, is a powerful tool for making a positive impact in the world. However, it's important to approach philanthropy thoughtfully and strategically in order to ensure that your giving is effective and meaningful. Here are some do's and don'ts of philanthropy:

DO's

1. **Do research and due diligence:** Before giving to a charity, it's important to research the organization and ensure that it is well-managed and making a real impact. Consult charity ratings organizations, such as Charity Navigator and GuideStar, to learn more about the organization's mission, finances, and impact.

2. **Do set specific, measurable goals:** Clearly defined goals will help you track the impact of your giving and determine if your philanthropic efforts are effective.

3. **Do involve others:** Philanthropy can be more effective and meaningful when shared with others. Involve family members, friends, or colleagues in the giving process, and find ways to make philanthropy a shared experience.

4. **Do give in a way that aligns with your values:** Giving to causes that align with your values will ensure that your philanthropy is more meaningful to you and that you are more likely to be engaged with the cause over the long-term.

5. **Do be strategic and take a long-term approach:** Strategic and long-term giving can help you maximize the impact of your donations and achieve your philanthropic goals more effectively.

DON'Ts

1. **Don't give impulsively:** Avoid giving to a charity simply because you've been solicited or because you feel guilty. Instead, take the time to research the organization and ensure that it aligns with your values and goals.

2. **Don't give too much too soon:** It's important to balance your philanthropic goals with your other financial obligations. Avoid overextending yourself financially and instead, develop a giving plan that is sustainable over time.

3. **Don't be afraid to ask questions:** If you have questions or concerns about an organization or its mission, don't be afraid to ask. A good charity should be able to provide clear and honest answers.

4. **Don't be afraid to change direction:** If you find that your giving is not making the impact that you had hoped for, don't be afraid to change direction and explore other giving opportunities.

5. **Don't forget to track the impact of your giving:** It's important to track the impact of your giving so you can evaluate the effectiveness of your philanthropy and make adjustments as necessary.

By following these do's and don'ts, you can ensure that your philanthropy is effective, meaningful, and truly makes a difference in the world. It's also important to remember that philanthropy is a personal endeavor and that there is no one-size-fits-all approach, so it's crucial to find what works best for you.

CHAPTER 10

Choosing the Right Financial Advisors Who Understand Philanthropy

Choosing the right financial advisor who understands philanthropy is crucial for maximizing the impact of your charitable giving. A financial advisor who has experience and expertise in philanthropy can provide valuable guidance and advice on how to make the most of your donations, and how to integrate your philanthropic goals with your overall financial plan.

When choosing a financial advisor, it's important to consider the following:

1. **Experience:** Look for an advisor who has experience working with philanthropic clients. This could include working with donors on charitable giving strategies, advising nonprofit organizations, or managing endowments.

2. **Expertise:** Make sure that your advisor has a deep understanding of philanthropy and the various giving options available. This includes knowledge of different types of charitable entities, such as private foundations, donor-advised funds, and charitable trusts.

3. **Network:** A good financial advisor will have a wide network of contacts in the philanthropic community, which can be invaluable for making connections and finding the right opportunities to support.

4. **Professionalism:** It's important to work with an advisor who is professional, responsive, and reliable. A good advisor will

be able to provide clear and honest advice, and will be responsive to your needs and questions.

5. **Values alignment**: It's important to work with an advisor who shares your values and understands your philanthropic goals. This will ensure that your advisor is fully committed to helping you achieve your goals.

It's also a good idea to ask for references and to speak with other clients who have worked with the advisor. Remember, choosing the right financial advisor is an important decision and it's worth taking the time to find the right one.

Working with a financial advisor who understands philanthropy can be a valuable asset in ensuring that your giving is strategic, effective, and impactful, and that it integrates well with your overall financial plan.

Common challenges of Philanthropy and How to Avoid Them

Philanthropy, the act of giving to charitable causes, can be a powerful tool for making a positive impact on society. However, it is not without its challenges. One of the most significant challenges is measuring the impact of donations and charitable giving. It can be difficult to determine whether a specific donation or initiative has had a meaningful impact on the intended cause. This challenge is further compounded by lack of transparency and accountability in the philanthropic sector. Many charitable organizations do not provide enough information about how donations are used or what impact they have, making it difficult for donors to make informed decisions about where to give.

Another challenge in philanthropy is the overhead costs associated with running a charitable organization. Many organizations have significant expenses, including administrative expenses, fundraising, and marketing costs. This can lead to a significant portion of donations being used for non-program expenses, which can be a concern for donors.

Philanthropy can also be challenged by a lack of coordination and collaboration among organizations working on similar issues or in the same geographic area. This can lead to inefficiencies and a lack of impact. Furthermore, philanthropy can be limited by the effectiveness of the programs being funded. Some programs may not be well-designed or implemented, or may not be appropriate for the target population, causing the philanthropic efforts to be ineffective.

Another challenge in philanthropy is the short-term focus that some philanthropic efforts may have. This means they don't consider long-term sustainability or scalability of their programs, which can limit the overall impact of philanthropy. There is also a lack of representation and cultural sensitivity in philanthropy, which can lead to inefficiencies and a lack of impact.

Finally, political and economic instability in certain areas can make it difficult for philanthropic organizations to operate and have a lasting impact. Despite these challenges, by addressing them, philanthropic organizations and donors can work together to make a greater impact on the causes they support. Philanthropy can be a powerful tool for making a positive impact on society, but it requires careful consideration, planning, and execution to maximize its potential.

Some common challenges include:

1. **Lack of focus:** Without a clear strategy or set of goals, philanthropy can become scattered and ineffective. To avoid this, it's important to research and choose causes that align with your values, and to take a strategic and long-term approach to giving.

2. **Inadequate due diligence:** Before giving to a charity, it's important to research the organization and ensure that it is well-managed and making a real impact. This can be done by consulting charity ratings organizations, such as Charity Navigator and GuideStar.

3. **Limited impact:** Simply giving money to a charity does not guarantee that it will be put to good use. To ensure that your donations are making a real difference, it's important to understand the organization's mission and goals, and to track the impact of your giving.

4. **Difficulty in evaluating the impact of your giving:** Many donors have a hard time measuring the impact of their giving, which can make it hard to determine if their philanthropic efforts are effective. To avoid this, it's important to set specific, measurable goals and to track progress towards those goals.

5. **Difficulty in engaging other family members or friends:** Philanthropy is often seen as a personal endeavor, but it can be more effective and meaningful when shared with others. To avoid this, it's important to involve other family members or friends in the giving process, and to find ways to make philanthropy a shared experience.

To avoid these challenges, it's important to be strategic and thoughtful in your giving, to do your research and due diligence, and to involve others in the process. By taking these steps, you can ensure that your philanthropy is effective, meaningful, and truly makes a difference in the world.

Where Can I Buy Wealth & Philanthropic Management Services?

An individual or organization may consider purchasing philanthropic management or consulting services for a variety of reasons. One potential reason is that they may not have the necessary expertise or resources to effectively manage their charitable giving. Philanthropic management and consulting firms can provide a wide range of services, such as strategic planning, grantmaking, and impact analysis, that can help an individual or organization make the most of their philanthropic efforts.

Another reason an individual or organization may consider purchasing philanthropic management or consulting services is that they may want to ensure that their giving aligns with their values and goals. Philanthropic management and consulting firms can help individuals and organizations identify the issues and causes that align with their values, and can also help them develop a giving strategy that will help them achieve their goals. They can also help individuals and organizations understand the impact of their giving, and can provide guidance on how to measure and evaluate that impact.

Here are several places where you can buy wealth and philanthropic management services. Some options include:

1. **Financial institutions:** Many banks and investment firms offer wealth management services that include philanthropic planning and advice.

2. **Philanthropic consulting firms:** These companies specialize in helping individuals and families plan and execute their charitable giving.

3. **Private foundations:** Some private foundations, such as community foundations, offer wealth management services in addition to their philanthropic services.

4. **Charity Navigator and GuideStar:** These are nonprofit organizations that provide information and ratings on charities, which can help you research and choose organizations to support.

5. **Online platforms:** There are several online platforms that provide information and resources to help you give smarter and more effectively.

It's important to research and compare different providers to find one that best meets your needs and aligns with your values. It's also a good idea to consult with a financial advisor or attorney to ensure that your philanthropic and wealth management goals are integrated and aligned with your overall financial plan.

Conclusion

In conclusion, "The Philanthropic Mindset: How to Give Smart and Live Rich" has provided readers with a comprehensive understanding of the benefits of a philanthropic mindset and how it can lead to a more fulfilling and meaningful life. The book has shown how individuals can give more effectively and maximize the impact of their donations, while also providing guidance on how to live a rich life by giving smartly and making a positive impact on the world. The book has highlighted the importance of research and due diligence when choosing a cause to support, as well as the benefits of taking a strategic and long-term approach to philanthropy. We hope that readers have been inspired to adopt a philanthropic mindset and make a difference in the world through their charitable giving. - Adella Pasos